Instant Raspberry Pi Gaming

Your guide to gaming on the Raspberry Pi, from classic arcade games to modern 3D adventures

Shea Silverman

PUBLISHING

BIRMINGHAM - MUMBAI

Instant Raspberry Pi Gaming

First published: September 2013

Production Reference: 1230913

Published by Packt Publishing Ltd.
Livery Place
35 Livery Street
Birmingham B3 2PB, UK.

ISBN 978-1-78328-323-1

www.packtpub.com

Credits

Author

Shea Silverman

Reviewers

Jacob Bates

Daniel O'Connor

Acquisition Editor

Owen Roberts

Commissioning Editor

Nikhil Chinnari

Technical Editor

Pratik More

Project Coordinator

Sherin Padayatty

Proofreader

Jonathan Todd

Production Coordinator

Manu Joseph

Cover Work

Manu Joseph

Cover Image

Abhinash Sahu

About the Author

Shea Silverman has been using computers since he was two years old. He has always been drawn to technology, video games, education, and the public sector. He is currently a member of the Orlando hackerspace FamiLAB, an alumni of the University of Central Florida, and is working toward his Masters in Non-profit Management. His article entitled *Hacking, Learning, and the Raspberry Pi* was published in *2600: The Hacker Quarterly*, and he was a technical reviewer for *Raspberry Pi Networking Cookbook*, also published by Packt Publishing.

You can find more information at http://www.sheasilverman.com.

I would like to thank my wonderful wife, Kristene, who provides unending encouragement and support for my projects. I would like to thank my friends and family for their ongoing support and finally Liz, Eben, and the Raspberry Pi Foundation for the creation of the Raspberry Pi, and the wonderful community that has flourished since its release.

About the Reviewers

Jacob Bates is a web developer at the University of Central Florida (UCF). He received his Bachelor's degree in Computer Engineering from UCF, and has continued to tinker with integrating hardware and software in his free time. He has developed software for the Arduino, Raspberry Pi, Android, and iOS platforms, including a Star Trek "Red Alert" system for his office.

Daniel O'Connor is an experienced developer and open data advocate, with more than eight years experience in a large variety of web and traditional software development paradigms, based in Adelaide, Australia.

Daniel works within the valuation and real property industry, having worked with key players such as RP Data, Valuation Exchange, and Herron Todd White to deliver innovative enterprise solutions.

When not at a day job, he can often be found participating in a large variety of open source work (`http://github.com/CloCkWeRX/`) and tinkering with his Raspberry Pi.

www.PacktPub.com

Support files, eBooks, discount offers, and more

You might want to visit www.PacktPub.com for support files and downloads related to your book.

Did you know that Packt Publishing offers eBook versions of every book published, with PDF and ePub files available? You can upgrade to the eBook version at www.PacktPub.com and as a print book customer, you are entitled to a discount on the eBook copy. Get in touch with us at service@packtpub.com for more details.

At www.PacktPub.com, you can also read a collection of free technical articles, sign up for a range of free newsletters, and receive exclusive discounts and offers on Packt Publishing books and eBooks.

http://PacktLib.PacktPub.com

Do you need instant solutions to your IT questions? PacktLib is Packt Publishing's online digital book library. Here, you can access, read, and search across Packt Publishing's entire library of books.

Why Subscribe?

- Fully searchable across every book published by Packt Publishing
- Copy and paste, print, and bookmark content
- On demand and accessible via web browser

Free Access for Packt Publishing account holders

If you have an account with Packt Publishing at www.PacktPub.com, you can use this to access PacktLib today and view nine entirely free books. Simply use your login credentials for immediate access.

Table of Contents

Preface

Since its introduction, the Raspberry Pi has spawned an enormous community, based around the $35 Linux computer. The device has created a huge hacking community, new business ventures, educational programs, student-learning opportunities, and of course, tons of gaming opportunities.

The Raspberry Pi is a powerful device, based around a 700 MHz ARM processor, 512 MB of RAM, HDMI and composite outputs, general purpose input/output pins, and a strong GPU. The idea of porting video games was formed even before release. One of the first demos was running Quake 3 Arena at 60 FPS. After that demo, a segment of the community focused on bringing over as many games as possible.

Now, there are multiple Raspberry Pi gaming distributions, one-step installers, official game ports from developers, and dozens of emulators available. The official Raspberry Pi App Store even has a section just for games.

With its low price point, large community, and vast amount of games, the Raspberry Pi is the perfect device for the gaming enthusiast.

What this book covers

Flashing your SD card (Simple) will teach you how to properly load various operating systems for your Raspberry Pi from the most common desktop software.

Connecting your Raspberry Pi (Simple) will introduce to you the various ways to set up a Raspberry Pi. It will primarily instruct you on how to set up the device for the optimal gaming environment.

Moving files to the Raspberry Pi (Intermediate) will explain and demonstrate the multiple ways to connect to the device, and transfer files from one system to the other. You will learn how to use USB flash drives, Secure Copy over SSH, and Linux file download tools such as `wget`.

Using the Raspberry Pi Store (Simple) will introduce and explain the different features of the official app store for the Raspberry Pi. You will create an account, log in, and download your first application.

Setting up PiMAME (Intermediate) is a collection of emulators and tools for gaming on the Raspberry Pi. You will be shown how to use the installer that will automatically download, set up, and configure the gaming environment for you, as well as how to use the tools and programs included in the collection.

Installing RetroPie (Intermediate) is a gaming platform for the Raspberry Pi that includes numerous emulators and games under one frontend. You will be taken through the steps of installing the program and running the various games.

Installing PiSNES (Intermediate) will show you how to install, launch, and play with an SNES emulator from the Pi Store.

Installing MAME4All (Intermediate) will show you how to install, launch, and play with a specially created version of MAME for the Raspberry Pi from the Pi Store.

Installing and running the PlayStation emulator (Advanced) will show you how to download, install, and run an advanced PlayStation emulator for the Raspberry Pi. It will guide you on how to load games, how the controls work, and what types of experiences are available.

Installing and running OpenArena (Simple) will show you how to install the free open source version of Quake 3 Arena. You will learn how to set up your character, play single-player games, connect to multiplayer matches, and run your own dedicated server.

Installing Cave Story (Simple) will explain how to download and launch the freeware platforming game Cave Story via its open source Linux port NXEngine.

Installing Stella (Simple) will show you how to use Linux's apt repository to install and run Stella, the multiplatform Atari 2600 emulator.

Using Minecraft Pi Edition (Advanced) will show you how to install and create your own Minecraft world, and then teach you how to extend it with Python and the Minecraft API.

Staying up-to-date (Intermediate) will show you how to keep your Raspberry Pi firmware and software updated using the included utilities.

Common troubleshooting (Intermediate) will help you fix common issues that crop up when starting out with your Raspberry Pi device.

What you need for this book

You will need a Raspberry Pi, a 5v 1amp Micro-USB power supply, HDMI or composite-enabled monitor, a 4 GB or larger SD card, network connection, a USB mouse and keyboard, and a computer running Linux, Mac OS X, or Windows.

You should also download the latest version of Raspbian, the official Raspberry Pi operating system, from `http://www.raspberrypi.org`. You need the version of Python that comes with Raspbian, and the Minecraft for Pi software available at `http://pi.minecraft.net/`.

Who this book is for

The target audience for this book is anyone who enjoys modern and retro gaming. You also shouldn't be afraid of playing on the cutting edge of hardware and software.

Conventions

In this book, you will find a number of styles of text that distinguish between different kinds of information. Here are some examples of these styles, and an explanation of their meaning.

Code words in text are shown as follows: "Move your game files into the `rom` folder in the `pisnes` directory."

New terms and **important words** are shown in bold. Words that you see on the screen, in menus or dialog boxes for example, appear in the text like this: "Click on the **My Library** tab."

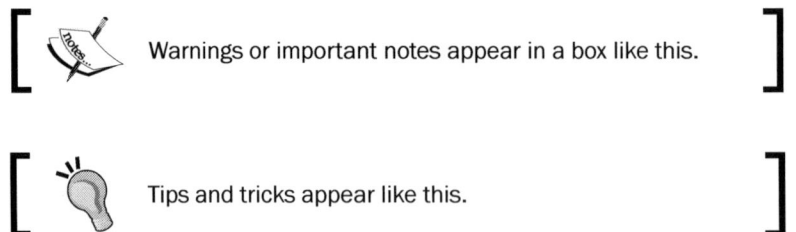

Warnings or important notes appear in a box like this.

Tips and tricks appear like this.

Reader feedback

Feedback from our readers is always welcome. Let us know what you think about this book—what you liked or may have disliked. Reader feedback is important for us to develop titles that you really get the most out of.

To send us general feedback, simply send an e-mail to feedback@packtpub.com, and mention the book title via the subject of your message.

If there is a topic that you have expertise in and you are interested in either writing or contributing to a book, see our author guide on www.packtpub.com/authors.

Customer support

Now that you are the proud owner of a Packt book, we have a number of things to help you to get the most from your purchase.

Downloading the example code

You can download the example code files for all Packt books you have purchased from your account at http://www.packtpub.com. If you purchased this book elsewhere, you can visit http://www.packtpub.com/support and register to have the files e-mailed directly to you.

Errata

Although we have taken every care to ensure the accuracy of our content, mistakes do happen. If you find a mistake in one of our books—maybe a mistake in the text or the code—we would be grateful if you would report this to us. By doing so, you can save other readers from frustration and help us improve subsequent versions of this book. If you find any errata, please report them by visiting http://www.packtpub.com/submit-errata, selecting your book, clicking on the **erratasubmissionform** link, and entering the details of your errata. Once your errata are verified, your submission will be accepted and the errata will be uploaded on our website, or added to any list of existing errata, under the Errata section of that title. Any existing errata can be viewed by selecting your title from http://www.packtpub.com/support.

Piracy

Piracy of copyright material on the Internet is an ongoing problem across all media. At Packt, we take the protection of our copyright and licenses very seriously. If you come across any illegal copies of our works, in any form, on the Internet, please provide us with the location address or website name immediately so that we can pursue a remedy.

Please contact us at copyright@packtpub.com with a link to the suspected pirated material.

We appreciate your help in protecting our authors, and our ability to bring you valuable content.

Questions

You can contact us at questions@packtpub.com if you are having a problem with any aspect of the book, and we will do our best to address it.

Instant Raspberry Pi Gaming

Welcome to *Instant Raspberry Pi Gaming*. The goal of this book is to bring you from a base installation to having a lot of fun as fast as possible. From classic arcade games to popular modern games, there will be something for everyone.

Flashing your SD card (Simple)

This task will explain how to prepare an SD card with a Linux-based Raspberry Pi operating system that can be created on Windows, Linux, and Mac OS X. The official operating system is **Raspbian** and we will be using that in the following section.

Getting ready

You will need:

- An SD card, class 4 or higher, between the sizes 4 GB and 32 GB
- An SD card reader connected to your computer
- A Raspbian Raspberry Pi operating system image
- Win32 Disk Imager (Windows Only)

How to do it...

Let's get started by downloading the latest version of Raspbian from
`http://www.raspberrypi.org/downloads`.

Before going any further, do keep this in mind:

 dd and Win32 Disk Imager can be used to overwrite your computer's own hard drive or other drives connected to your computer. Double and triple check that the drive you are selecting is your SD card.

Here are the steps for the following operating systems:

Microsoft Windows

1. Unzip the Raspbian image by double-clicking on the `Raspbian.zip` file.

2. Select a place on your hard drive to save the extracted file.

3. Click on **Extract**.

4. Insert the SD card into your computer's SD card reader.

5. Run `Win32 Disk Imager`.

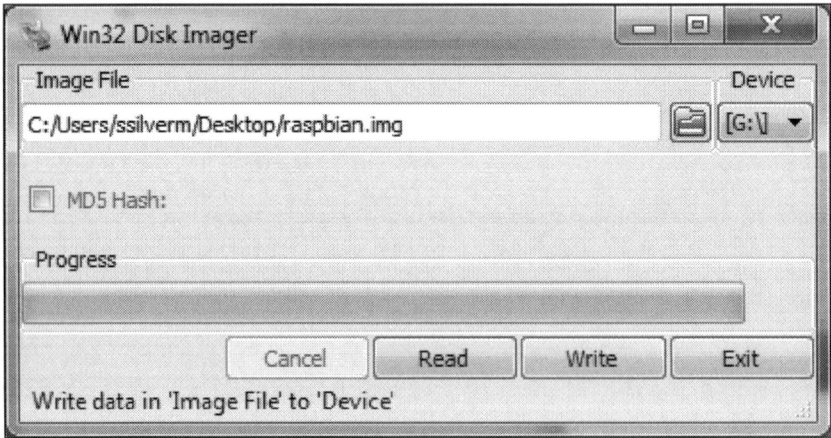

6. Select the Raspberry Pi image on your hard drive.

7. Select the drive letter under the device that corresponds to the SD card.

8. Click on the **Write** button.

Mac OS X

1. Double-click on the Raspbian image ZIP file. It will automatically extract into the same place as the ZIP file.

2. Insert the SD card into your computer's SD card reader.

3. Open the terminal application (by navigating to **Applications | Utilities folder**).

4. Find the name of your SD card by typing `diskutil list`.

```
C02FV3EJDF91:~ shea$ diskutil list
/dev/disk0
   #:                       TYPE NAME                    SIZE       IDENTIFIER
   0:      GUID_partition_scheme                        *121.3 GB   disk0
   1:                        EFI                          209.7 MB   disk0s1
   2:                  Apple_HFS Macintosh HD             120.5 GB   disk0s2
   3:                 Apple_Boot Recovery HD              650.0 MB   disk0s3
/dev/disk1
   #:                       TYPE NAME                    SIZE       IDENTIFIER
   0:      GUID_partition_scheme                        *320.1 GB   disk1
   1:                        EFI                          209.7 MB   disk1s1
   2:        Microsoft Basic Data BOOTCAMP               127.7 GB   disk1s2
/dev/disk2
   #:                       TYPE NAME                    SIZE       IDENTIFIER
   0:     FDisk_partition_scheme                         *2.0 GB    disk2
   1:              Windows_FAT_32 boot                    58.7 MB    disk2s1
   2:                      Linux                          1.9 GB     disk2s2
C02FV3EJDF91:~ shea$ ▊
```

5. Unmount your SD card by typing `disktuil umountdisk <disk>`, that is, `/dev/disk2`.

```
C02FV3EJDF91:~ shea$ diskutil umountdisk /dev/disk2
Unmount of all volumes on disk2 was successful
C02FV3EJDF91:~ shea$ ▊
```

6. Copy the OS image on your hard drive to the SD card by typing `dd if=/path/to/os/image.img of=<disk>`, that is, `/dev/disk2`.

7. It can take anywhere from 15 minutes to more than an hour for the image to be written to the SD card. It appears as if nothing is happening until it finishes copying. When it has completed, you will see a message showing how long it took to transfer, in seconds.

```
C02FV3EJDF91:~ shea$ dd if=/Users/shea/raspbian.img of=/dev/disk2
3788800+0 records in
3788800+0 records out
1939865600 bytes transferred in 1837.087116 secs (1055946 bytes/sec)
C02FV3EJDF91:~ shea$ ▊
```

Linux

1. Insert the SD card into your computer's SD card reader.

2. Using the terminal of your system, find the name of your SD card by typing `sudo fdisk -l`.

3. If needed, unmount your SD card by typing `umount <disk>`, that is, `/dev/disk3`.

4. Copy the OS image on your hard drive to the SD card by typing `dd if=/path/to/os/image.img of=<disk>`.

How it works...

The Raspberry Pi is designed to start up from a bootable SD card. The Raspbian image file has already been set up for the Raspberry Pi to properly boot and run the Linux operating system. Unlike copying the file straight to the SD card, Win32 Disk Imager and `dd` copies what is inside the image file to the SD card at a bit-for-bit level.

There's more...

Few useful reference links:

- For information on Raspberry Pi Operating Systems go to `http://www.raspberrypi.org/downloads`

- For information on Raspbian go to `http://www.raspbian.org`

- For information on Win32 Disk Imager go to `http://sourceforge.net/projects/win32diskimager/`

- For information on dd go to `http://en.wikipedia.org/wiki/Dd_(Unix)`

- For information on fdisk go to `http://en.wikipedia.org/wiki/Fdisk`

- For information on diskutil go to `http://en.wikipedia.org/wiki/Disk_Utility`

Connecting your Raspberry Pi (Simple)

This task will demonstrate how to set up Raspberry Pi properly. This will include High-Definition Multimedia Interface (HDMI), Composite TVs, keyboards and mice, and networking.

Getting ready

You will need:

- A Raspberry Pi
- A 5 volt 1 amp power adapter with a Micro-USB connector
- An SD card with a Raspberry Pi operating system installed
- An Ethernet cable with a network connection
- One HDMI cable or RCA style (composite) cable
- A USB keyboard
- A USB mouse

How to do it...

1. Place your SD card into the SD card slot on the underside of the Raspberry Pi.

2. Connect the HDMI or RCA cable to the respective connector on the Raspberry Pi, and plug the other end into your monitor.

3. Plug the Ethernet cable into the Ethernet jack on the Raspberry Pi and the other end into your router or switch.

4. Connect the USB mouse and keyboard to the two USB ports available on the Raspberry Pi.

5. Plug the power supply's Micro-USB connector into the Micro-USB port on the Raspberry Pi to turn it on.

6. A red LED by the USB ports will light up, indicating power.

7. On your screen, a square rainbow image will appear for a brief moment, followed by some quick moving text or a graphic loading screen.

8. At this point you have successfully booted up your Raspberry Pi.

How it works...

The Raspberry Pi is a small, embedded computer with many of the same components and connectors that you would find on a larger desktop system. A bare minimum Raspberry Pi setup requires only an SD card and a power supply for proper functioning. Adding an Ethernet cable allows you to connect to the Raspberry Pi via Secure Shell (SSH) and to the Internet. Adding a monitor and USB keyboard/mouse allows you to use the Raspberry Pi like most common desktop computer systems.

Moving files to the Raspberry Pi (Intermediate)

This task will describe how to:

▶ Copy files from a flash drive to the SD card

▶ Download files from a remote site

▶ Use the local network to transfer files from a computer to the Raspberry Pi

Getting ready

You will need:

- A Raspberry Pi
- An SD card with the official Raspberry Pi OS, Raspbian, properly loaded
- A USB keyboard
- A USB mouse
- A USB flash drive
- A 5V 1A power supply with Micro-USB connector
- A network connection
- Optional: powered USB hub
- And a screen hooked up to your Raspberry Pi

How to do it...

For downloading from a remote site, perform the following steps:

1. Copy down the URL address of the file you want to download.
2. From the command line, enter `wget http://example.com/link/to/file/filename`.
3. The file will be downloaded to the current folder on your Raspberry Pi.

For copying from a flash drive, perform the following steps:

1. From the command line enter `startx` to load GUI.
2. Insert your USB flash drive into one of the available USB ports.
3. Select **Open in File Manager** from the pop-up window and click on **Ok**.
4. From the File Manager you can drag-and-drop files between the USB drive and SD card.

For copying using FileZilla and SCP/SFTP, perform the following steps:

1. Download and install FileZilla.

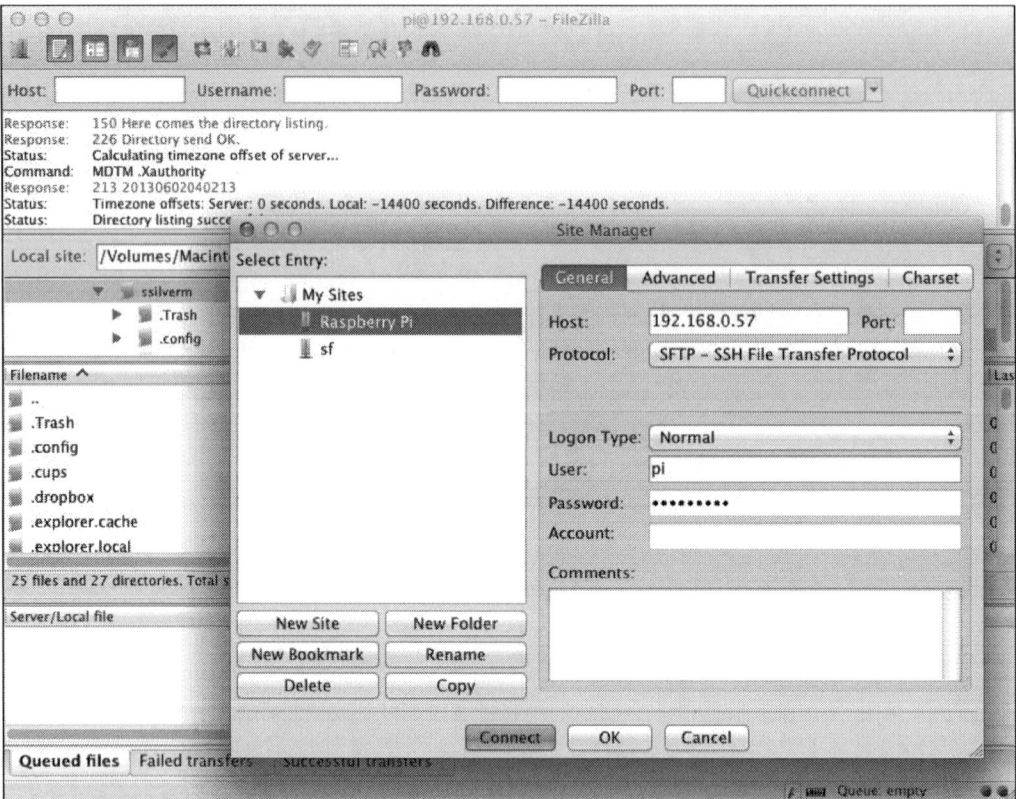

2. With FileZilla open, go to the **File** menu and select **Site Manager**.

3. Click on the **New Site** button, and enter in a name for the newly created item.

4. In the **Host** text box, enter the IP address of your Raspberry Pi.

    1. The easiest way to find out your Raspberry Pi's IP is by watching Raspbian boot up. Above the login prompt will be a message displaying your current IP address.

    2. You can also find out the IP of your device by typing `ifconfig` at the command line and pressing *Enter*. Your IP will be displayed next to `eth0`.

5. From the **Protocol** drop-down menu select **SFTP - SSH File Transfer Protocol**.

6. From the **Logon Type** drop-down menu select **Normal**.

7. Enter in your Raspberry Pi's username and password (default: `pi` / `raspberry`) and then click on the **Connect** button.

8. After a moment, you will be connected to your Raspberry Pi and viewing the files in the Pi's user home directory, `/home/pi`.

9. You can now create new folders and drag-and-drop files between your computer and the Raspberry Pi.

How it works...

wget is a powerful tool for downloading numerous items from the Internet or a local network. The simplest way of using it is by just giving it a URL, and wget will try to download the item to the same folder in which it is running.

The desktop environment provides a modern experience akin to using Windows or Mac OS X. When you insert a USB flash drive, the GUI recognizes a new device that has been inserted and automatically mounts and configures the drive for use. From this point onward, you can use the file manager to drag-and-drop files between the Raspberry Pi's storage and your flash drive.

FileZilla is a popular open source file transfer application. By default, Raspbian ships with SSH-enabled SCP and SFTP allows files to be transferred over the SSH protocol. FileZilla supports SCP and SFTP out of the box. When you connect to the Raspberry Pi using SFTP, you are using SSH and SCP for securely and efficiently moving files from one place to the other.

There's more...

A few useful reference links:

▸ For information on wget go to `http://www.gnu.org/software/wget/`

▸ For information on LXDE go to `http://lxde.org/`

▸ For downloading and information on FileZilla go to `https://filezilla-project.org/`

▸ For information on SSH go to `http://en.wikipedia.org/wiki/Secure_Shell`

▸ For information on SCP go to `http://en.wikipedia.org/wiki/Secure_copy`

▸ For information on SFTP go to `http://en.wikipedia.org/wiki/SSH_File_Transfer_Protocol`

▸ For information on Ifconfig go to `http://en.wikipedia.org/wiki/Ifconfig`

Using the Raspberry Pi Store (Simple)

This will explain how to load up the Raspberry Pi App Store, how to set up an account, and how to search and install applications.

Getting ready

You will need:

▸ A Raspberry Pi

▸ An SD card with the official Raspberry Pi OS, Raspbian, properly loaded

▸ A USB keyboard

▸ A USB mouse

▸ A 5V 1A power supply with Micro-USB connector

▸ A network connection

▸ And a screen hooked up to your Raspberry Pi

How to do it...

1. At the command line, enter `startx` to start the desktop environment.
2. On the desktop, double-click on the Pi Store icon.
3. Click on the **Log In** link in the top-right of the window, as shown in the following screenshot:

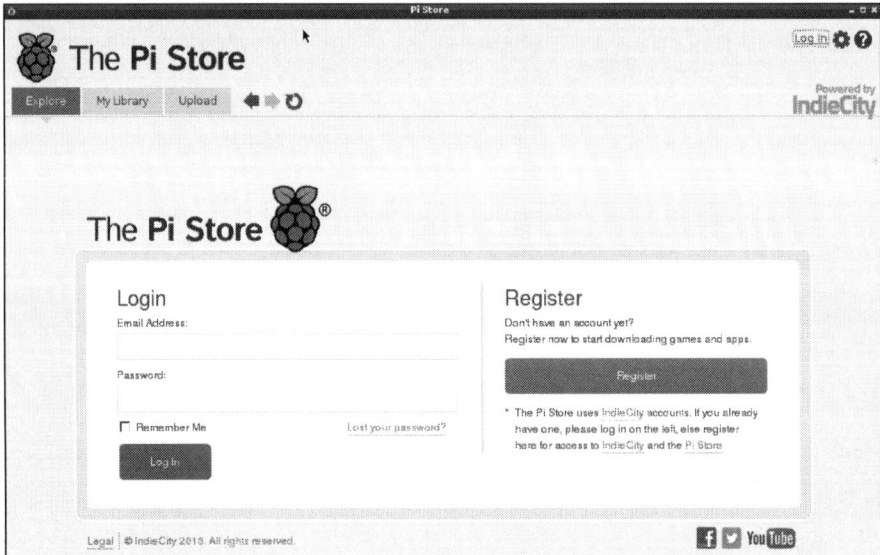

4. If you have not set up one yet, create an account now, and then log in with the e-mail address and password you used for registration.

5. You can search for software using the search bar or click on a category to bring up applications and games specific to that area.

6. Click on the **Download** and/or **Purchase** button when you have found a selection you like to add it to your library.

7. The selected item will be downloaded and automatically installed.

8. In the **My Library** tab, click on the item you want to run, and then click the **Launch** button.

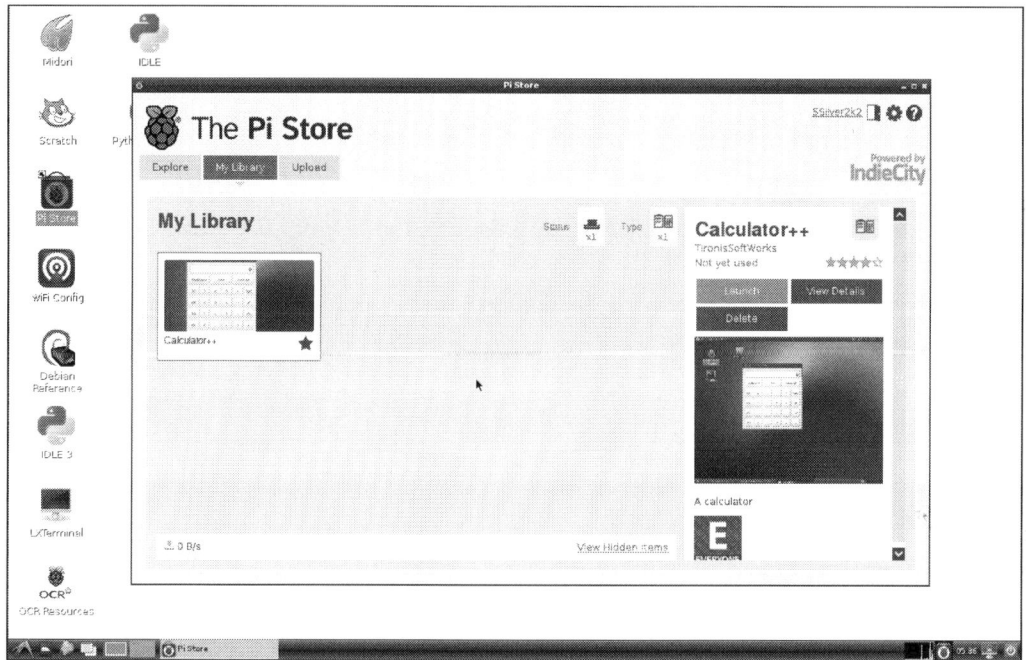

How it works...

The Raspberry Pi Store is an application that is installed by default on the latest versions of Raspbian. Developers can sign up and upload their games to the store. Pricing for games starts at free and can go up from there. Once the game has been made available on the store, any user with an account can purchase it. All available purchases will be available through the store on any Raspberry Pi you log in to. All games and apps are stored under the /usr/ local/bin/indiecity folder for playing offline.

There's more...

Here are a few useful reference links:

- ▸ The Pi Store's website: `http://store.raspberrypi.com/projects`
- ▸ Indiecity: `http://store.indiecity.com/`

Setting up PiMAME (Intermediate)

This task will guide you on how to download, install, and use **PiMAME** on your Raspberry Pi. You will learn how to add games into the proper directories, and using the PiMAME menu to launch the emulators. Finally, you will be introduced to the PiMAME web frontend. PiMAME currently emulates MAME, NeoGeo, SNES, and PlayStation systems.

Getting ready

You will need:

- ▸ A Raspberry Pi
- ▸ An SD card with the official Raspberry Pi OS, Raspbian, properly loaded
- ▸ A USB keyboard
- ▸ A USB mouse
- ▸ A 5V 1A power supply with Micro-USB connector
- ▸ A network connection
- ▸ And a screen hooked up to your Raspberry Pi

How to do it...

For installing PiMAME, perform the following steps:

1. At the command prompt, enter `sudo apt-get update`.
2. When that is complete, enter `sudo apt-get install git`.
3. Once apt-get has finished installing git, enter in `git clone https://github.com/ssilverm/pimame_installer`.
4. After git has finished cloning `pimame_installer` to your system, enter `cd pimame_installer` to move into that directory.
5. Type in `./install.sh` and press *Enter*.
6. Once the installation has finished, reboot your Raspberry Pi. PiMAME is now installed.

For using PiMAME, enter the following steps:

1. Move your game files into the respective subfolder in `/home/pi/roms/`.

2. The PiMAME menu will load at each boot-up.

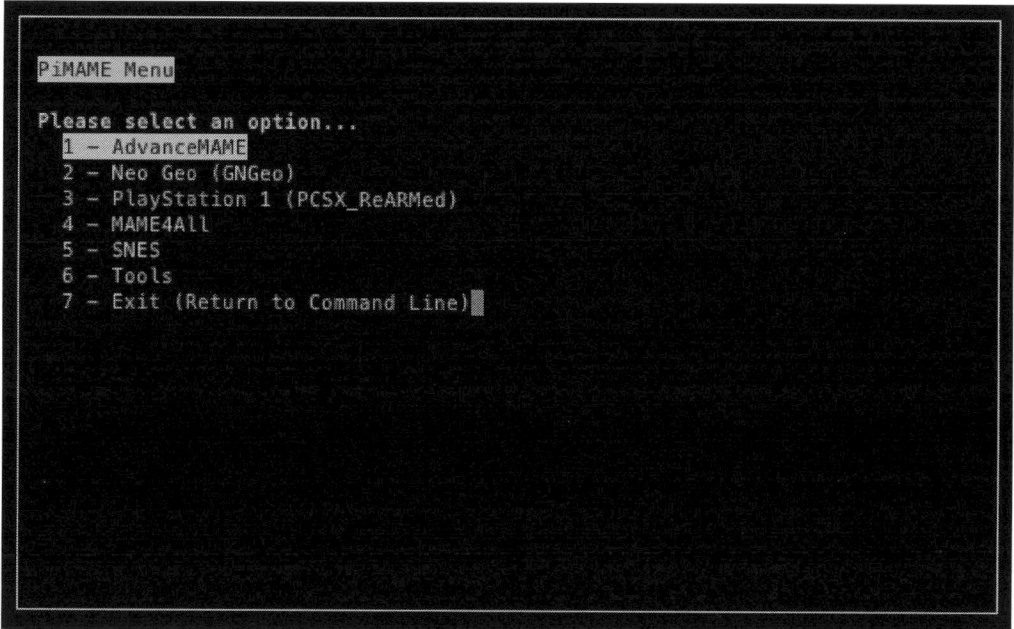

3. Use the arrow keys on your keyboard to move up and down the menu.

4. Press *return* to select the highlighted option.

5. When selected, each emulator will scan its folder for the proper game files and display them in a game menu.

6. From the game menu, use the arrow keys to select a game, and press *Enter* to play the selection.

7. When you are finished, press *Esc* to exit back to the menu.

For using the PiMAME web frontend, perform the following steps:

1. From a web browser on your computer, enter the Raspberry Pi's IP address into the URL bar and press *Enter*.

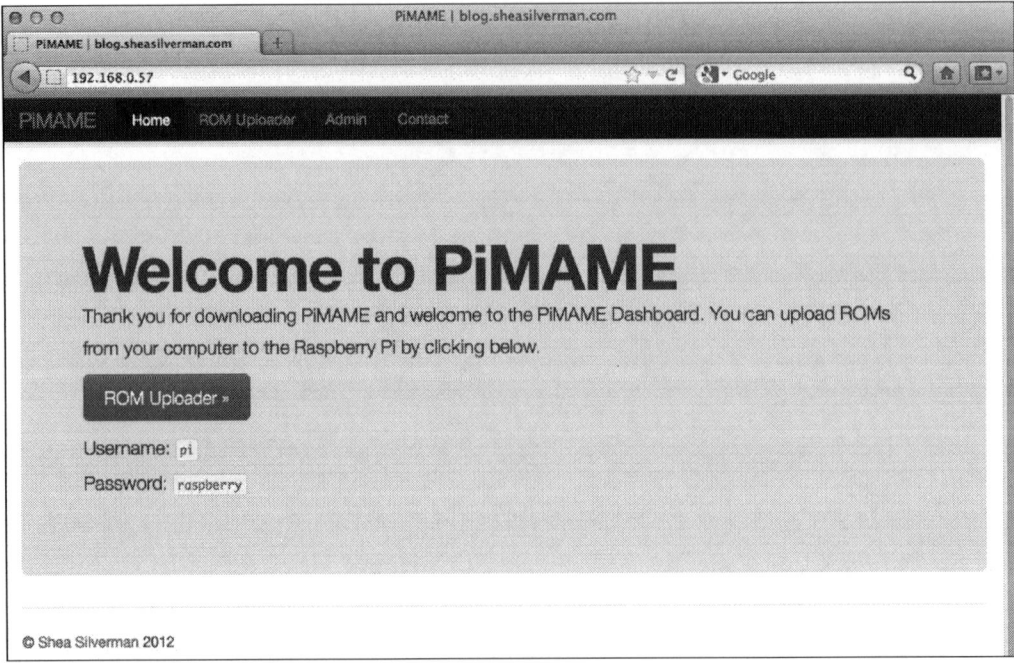

2. To upload files with PiMAME, select **Rom Uploader** from the PiMAME welcome screen.
3. Enter your username and password (default is `pi / raspberry`).

4. Select the directory where you wish to upload files.

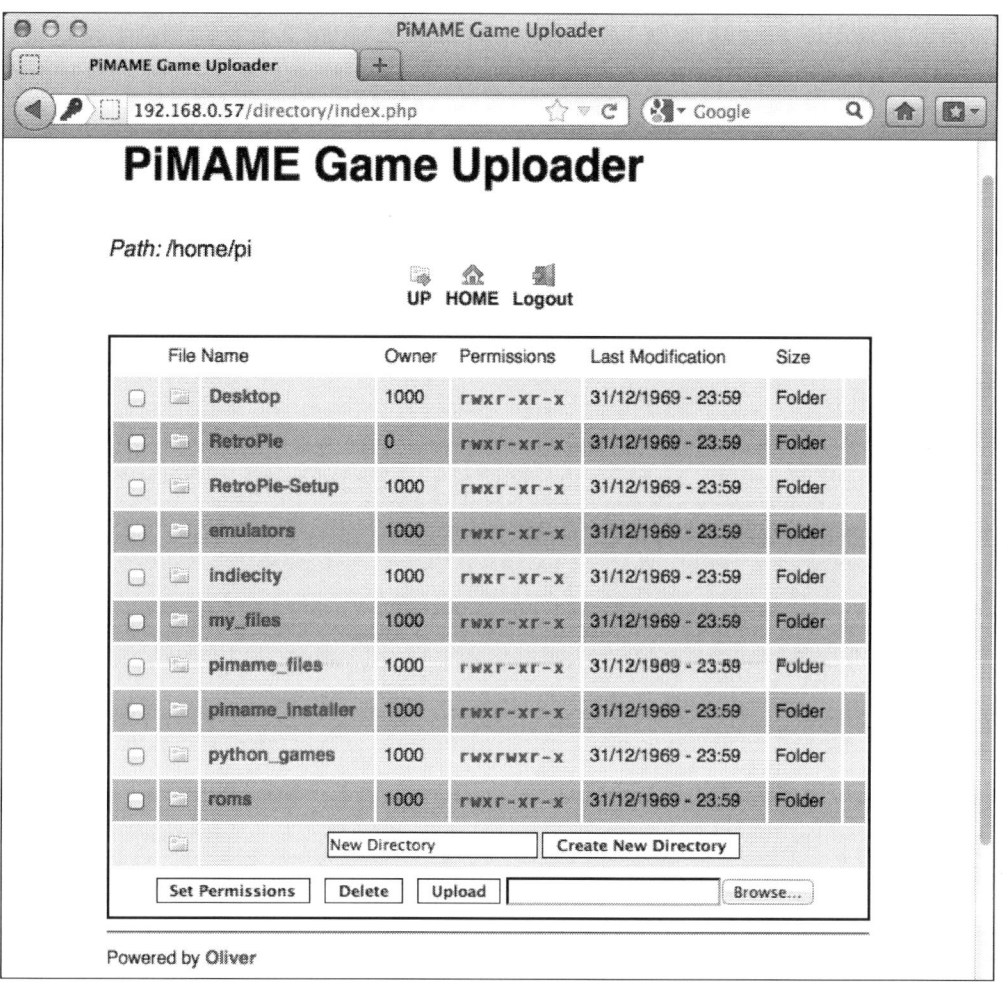

5. Click on the **Browse...** button and select a file to upload.

6. Click on the **Upload** button.

7. After a few moments, the file will be transferred to your Raspberry Pi.

8. To reboot or shutdown your Raspberry Pi using PiMAME, go back to the welcome screen and select **Admin** at the top menu bar.

9. Click on either **Reboot** or **Shutdown**.

10. Your Raspberry Pi is now rebooting or shutting down.

For updating PiMAME, perform the following steps:

1. On the command line, enter `cd ~/pimame_installer`.

2. Run the updater by entering `./update.sh` and wait for it to finish.

3. Reboot your Raspberry Pi.

How it works...

PiMAME is a combination of numerous tools, applications, and scripts that have been wrapped together to form a cohesive gaming experience on the Raspberry Pi. The install script launches apt-get and installs updates and device libraries that allow the other applications to run. Afterward, the PiMAME config files are cloned from a git repository, and the emulators are downloaded from their respective sites using wget. Once all the downloads are completed, the emulators are installed, the PiMAME config files are placed in the proper folders, the menu is set to launch at bootup, and the login settings are set to auto login.

With PiMAME installed, every time you boot up your Raspberry Pi, you will automatically be logged in and presented with the PiMAME menu. From here you can access the pre-installed emulators and other options.

PiMAME includes a built-in web frontend / control panel that is accessed through your web browser. Enter in your Raspberry Pi's IP address into the URL bar of your browser, and the welcome page should appear. The frontend includes a file uploader and file manager. The frontend also provides the ability to reboot and shutdown your Raspberry Pi.

The update script downloads the latest PiMAME files, which then brings all the files and emulators to the latest version. The updater checks for user modifications to the configuration files, and backs them, so the user won't lose custom settings.

There's more...

Here are a few useful reference links:

▶ For PiMAME project go to `http://www.pimame.org`

▶ For information on git go to `http://git-scm.com/`

Installing RetroPie (Intermediate)

This task will start by guiding you on how to download and install the **RetroPie** project. You will then learn how to add games and run the RetroPie frontend, EmulationStation. RetroPie currently emulates and runs MAME, Genesis, Super NES, NES, PSX, GameBoy, NXEngine, Apple][, x86, Duke Nukem 3D, and Doom games.

Getting ready

You will need:

▸ A Raspberry Pi

▸ An SD card with the official Raspberry Pi OS, Raspbian, properly loaded

▸ A USB keyboard

▸ A USB mouse

▸ A 5V 1A power supply with Micro-USB connector

▸ A network connection

▸ And a screen hooked up to your Raspberry Pi

How to do it...

For installing RetroPie, perform the following steps:

1. At the command line, enter `sudo apt-get update`.

2. Next, type `sudo apt-get install git dialog`.

3. Now enter `git clone https://github.com/petrockblog/RetroPie-Setup`.

4. Change directories to the newly created RetroPie setup by entering `cd RetroPie-Setup/`.

5. Enter `chmod +x retropie_setup.sh`.

6. Enter `sudo ./retropie_setup.sh`.

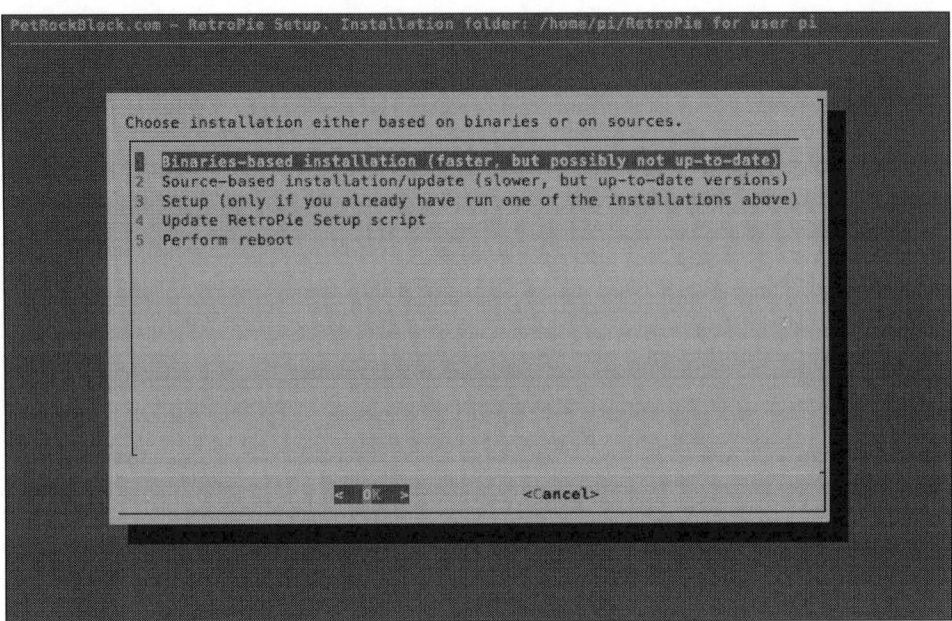

7. Choose the binaries-based installation from the installation screen and wait for the setup process to finish.

8. Once the installation has finished, select **Perform Reboot**.

For using RetroPie, perform the following steps:

1. Move your game files into the respective subfolders in `/home/pi/RetroPie/roms/`.

2. To use RetroPie, type `emulationstation` into your command line.

3. Use the up and down arrows keys to move between the list of games.

4. Use the left and right arrows to select between emulators.

5. To exit out of a game, press the *Esc* key.

6. Press *F1* to bring up the frontend menu, which will allow you to exit, change settings, or reboot, or *F4* to exit to the console.

How it works...

RetroPie is a tightly integrated set of scripts and applications, based around the open source RetroArch project and the **Emulationstation** frontend. **RetroArch**, also called libretro, is a portable set of *cores* that allow the emulation of various systems and games.

Emulationstation is a GUI frontend for selecting multiple games and systems. It takes advantage of the Raspberry Pi's video core for smooth transitions and fast rendering of menus with numerous games installed.

There's more...

Here are a few useful reference links:

▶ For information on RetroArch go to `http://libretro.org`

▶ For information on Emulationstation go to
`https://github.com/Aloshi/EmulationStation`

Installing PiSNES (Intermediate)

This task will describe how to install **PiSNES** through the Raspberry Pi Store, and how to install PiSNES from the Google Code site. It will go on to explain how to run it from both the Graphical User Interface (GUI) and the Command Line Interface (CLI), and how to add games.

Getting ready

You will need:

▶ A Raspberry Pi

▶ An SD card with the official Raspberry Pi OS, Raspbian, properly loaded

▶ A USB keyboard

▶ A USB mouse

▶ A 5V 1A power supply with Micro-USB connector

▶ A network connection

▶ And a screen hooked up to your Raspberry Pi

How to do it...

For installing PiSNES from the Pi Store, perform the following steps:

1. From the command line, enter `startx` to launch the desktop environment.

2. From the desktop, launch the Pi Store application by double-clicking on the Pi Store icon.

3. At the top-right of the application, there will be a **Log In** link. Click on the link and log in with your registered account.

4. Type `pisnes` in the search bar and press *Enter*.

5. Click on the `PiSNES` result.

6. At the application info page, click on the **Download** button on the right-hand side of the screen.

7. PiSNES will automatically start the download process, and a window will appear showing the installation process.

8. Press any button to close the window once it has finished installation.

9. PiSNES will look for your game files in the `/usr/local/bin/indiecity/InstalledApps/pisnes/Full/roms` directory.

For running PiSNES from the Pi Store, perform the following steps:

1. From the desktop, launch the Pi Store application by double-clicking on the Pi Store icon.

2. At the top right of the application, there will be a login link. Click on the link and log in with your registered account.

3. Click on the **My Library** tab.

4. Click on **PiSNES** and then click on **Launch**.

For running PiSNES from the command line, perform the following steps:

1. Type `cd /usr/local/bin/indiecity/InstalledApps/pisnes/Full` and press *Enter*.

2. Type `./snes9x.gui` and press *Enter* to launch PiSNES.

For installing and running PiSNES from Google Code, perform the following steps:

1. At the command line, type `wget https://pisnes.googlecode.com/files/pisnes%202013-05-25.zip -o pisnes.zip`.

2. Type `unzip pisnes.zip` and press *Enter*.

3. Type `cd pisnes` and press *Enter* to enter the PiSNES directory.

4. Move your game files into the `rom` folder in the `pisnes` directory.

5. Type `./snes9x.gui` and press *Enter* to launch PiSNES.

How it works...

PiSNES is a **Super Nintendo Entertainment System** emulator, based on the SNES9x project, and optimized to use the Raspberry Pi graphics processor. PiSNES uses an older version of the SNES9x codebase, which means that games which require emulation of the SuperFX will not run. The reason for this is that the newer versions of SNES9x have sacrificed speed for accuracy. When emulators are written, it usually starts off by getting a system running well enough to play, and as new versions are released, bugs are squashed, accuracy is improved, and more computing power is needed to emulate the hardware at full speed. By using an older version of SNES9x code, PiSNES is able to play a large amount of games at full speed, with a small chance that the audio and graphics may be a bit on the lower side.

The default controls for PiSNES are:

▶ **Arrow Keys**: These are equal to the D-pad

▶ *return*: This is equal to the *start* button

▶ *Tab*: This is equal to the *select* button

- ▸ *Esc*: This is equal to quit
- ▸ *D*: This is equal to the *a* button
- ▸ *C*: This is equal to the *b* button
- ▸ *S*: This is equal to the *x* button
- ▸ *X*: This is equal to the *y* button
- ▸ *A*: This is equal to the left bumper button
- ▸ *F*: This is equal to the right bumper button

You can modify these keys and other configuration options by editing the `snes9x.cfg` file.

There's more...

A few useful reference links:

- ▸ For PiSNES project go to `http://code.google.com/p/pisnes/`
- ▸ For SNES9x project go to `http://www.snes9x.com/`

Installing MAME4All (Intermediate)

This task will describe how to install MAME4All through the Raspberry Pi Store. It will also explain how to run it from both the GUI and the CLI, and how to add games.

Getting ready

You will need:

- ▸ A Raspberry Pi
- ▸ An SD card with the official Raspberry Pi OS, Raspbian, properly loaded
- ▸ A USB keyboard
- ▸ A USB mouse
- ▸ A 5V 1A power supply with Micro-USB connector
- ▸ A network connection
- ▸ And a screen hooked up to your Raspberry Pi

How to do it...

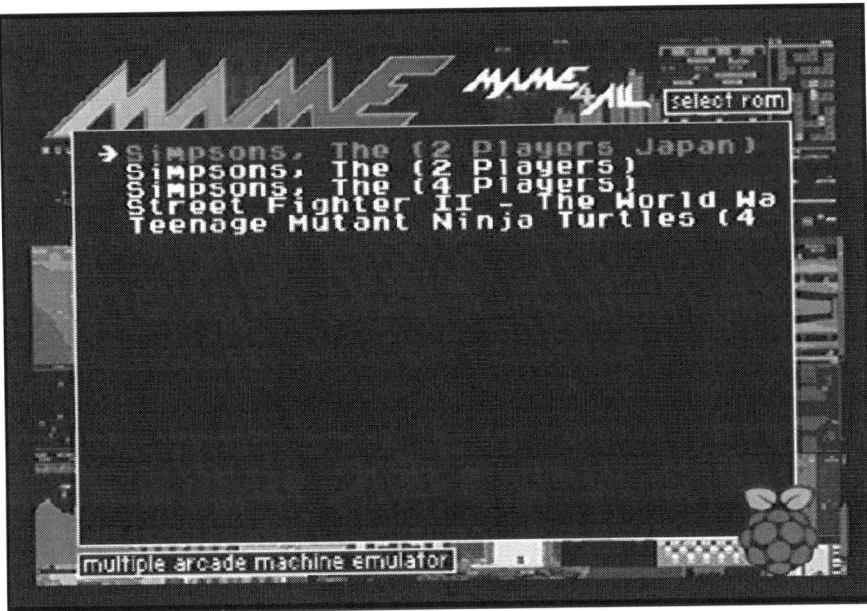

Perform the following steps for installing MAME4All:

1. From the command line, enter `startx` to launch the desktop environment.

2. From the desktop, launch the Pi Store application by double-clicking on the Pi Store icon.

3. At the top-right of the application, there will be a **Log In** link. Click on this link and log in with your registered account.

4. Type `MAME4All` in the search bar, and press *Enter*.

5. Click on the MAME4All result.

6. At the application's information page, click on the **Download** button on the right-hand side of the screen.

7. MAME4All will automatically download, and a window will appear showing the installation process.

8. Press any button to close the window once it has finished installing.

9. MAME4All will look for your game files in the `/usr/local/bin/indiecity/InstalledApps/MAME4ALL-pi/Full/roms` directory.

Perform the following steps for running MAME4All from the Pi Store:

1. From the desktop, launch the Pi Store application by double-clicking on the Pi Store icon.

2. At the top-right of the application, there will be a **Log In** link. Click on the link and log in with your registered account.

3. Click on the **My Library** tab.

4. Click on **MAME4All**, and then click on **Launch**.

For running MAME4All from the command line, perform the following steps:

1. Type `cd /usr/local/bin/indiecity/InstalledApps/mame4all_pi/Full` and press *Enter*.

2. Type `./mame` and press *Enter* for launching MAME4All.

How it works...

MAME4All is a **Multi Arcade Machine Emulator** that takes advantage of the Raspberry Pi's GPU to achieve very fast emulation of arcade machines. It is able to achieve this speed by compiling with DispManX, which offloads SDL code to the graphics core via OpenGL ES. When you run MAME4All, it looks for any game files you have in the `roms` directory and displays them in a menu for you to select from. If it doesn't find any files, it exits after a few seconds.

The default keys for MAME4All-Pi are:

▸ *5* for inserting coins

▸ *1* for player 1 to start

▸ Arrow keys for player 1 joystick controls

▸ *Ctrl*, *Alt*, space bar, *Z*, *X*, and *C* for default action keys

You can modify the MAME4All configuration by editing the `/usr/local/bin/indiecity/InstalledApps/mame4all_pi/Full/mame.cfg` file.

There's more...

A few useful reference links:

▸ For information on MAME project go to `http://mamedev.org/`

▸ For information on MAME4All project go to `http://code.google.com/p/mame4all-pi/`

Installing and running the PlayStation emulator (Advanced)

This task will describe how to download and copy PCSX ReARMed, the PlayStation emulator, to the Raspberry Pi. It will also explain how to run it from the CLI, how to change configuration settings, how games need to be loaded, and the controls.

Getting ready

You will need:

- A Raspberry Pi
- An SD card with the official Raspberry Pi OS, Raspbian, properly loaded
- A USB keyboard
- A USB mouse
- A 5V 1A power supply with Micro-USB connector
- A network connection
- And a screen hooked up to your Raspberry Pi

How to do it...

For installing PCSX ReARMed, perform the following steps:

1. You will need to have the Raspberry Pi desktop environment running for this recipe. If you are at the command line, type `startx` to launch the desktop environment.
2. On the desktop, launch the Pi Store application by double-clicking on the Pi Store icon.
3. At the top-right of the application, there will be a **Log In** link. Click on it and log in with your registered account.
4. Once logged in, type in `PCSX ReARMed` in the search bar.
5. Click on the PCSX ReARMed result that appears. Doing so will bring you to the application info page.
6. From here, click on the **Download** button on the right-hand side of the screen.
7. You will be brought to the **My Library** tab that will list all of your current applications. PCSX ReARMed will automatically download, and a window will appear showing the installation process. Press any button to close the window once it has finished installation.
8. To run PCSX ReARMed, click on the application in the **My Library** tab, and then click on **Launch**.

For running PCSX_ReARMed from the command line, perform the following steps:

1. Change into the `pcsx_rearmed` directory with the command `cd /usr/local/bin/indiecity/InstalledApps/pcsx_rearmed/Full/`.
2. Type `./pcsx` and press *Enter*.
3. The PCSX info message and menu should appear.

For running a game, perform the following steps:

1. From the main menu, use the up and down arrow keys to highlight **Load Game** and press *Enter*. You will be brought to either the previous directory you were in, or the `/media` drive.

2. You can move to a parent directory by selecting `./` and into a directory by selecting the directory name and pressing *Enter*.
3. Select the game file you want to run and hit *Enter*.
4. After a moment, the game will load.

How it works...

PCSX ReARMed is a port of the PCSX project to ARM processors and OpenGL ES compatible GPUs. PCSX ReARMed has been compiled to take advantage of the Raspberry Pi's architecture, and is capable of loading PlayStation games from the original disks using a USB CD-ROM drive, CD-ROM images, or independently developed images. For ease of use and speed, CD-ROM images are the preferred format.

The control scheme is as follows:

- Arrow keys to move
- *G* for triangle
- *X* for circle
- *Z* for cross
- *S* for square
- *W* for L1
- *R* for R1
- *E* for L2
- *L* for R2
- *V* for start
- *C* for select

There's more...

The PlayStation console was once a very powerful 3D console with a huge install base. Emulation of the console was a high priority, and was even turned into commercial projects, such as Bleem, a PlayStation emulator for the DreamCast, and Connectix Virtual Game Station, a PlayStation emulator for the Macintosh.

A few useful reference links:

- For information on PCSX ReARMed go to
  `https://github.com/notaz/pcsx_rearmed`
- For information on PCSX go to `http://www.pcsx.net/`
- For information on Sony PlayStation go to
  `http://en.wikipedia.org/wiki/PlayStation_%28console%29`
- For information on Bleem go to `http://en.wikipedia.org/wiki/Bleem!`
- For information on Connectix VGS go to
  `http://en.wikipedia.org/wiki/Connectix_Virtual_Game_Station`

Installing and running OpenArena (Simple)

This task will describe how to install OpenArena through the Raspberry Pi Store. It will go on to explain how to run it, setting up your character, playing a single-player game, joining multiplayer games, and setting up a multiplayer server.

Getting ready

You will need:

- A Raspberry Pi
- An SD card with the official Raspberry Pi OS, Raspbian, properly loaded
- A USB keyboard
- A USB mouse
- A 5V 1A power supply with Micro-USB connector
- A network connection
- And a screen hooked up to your Raspberry Pi

How to do it...

For installing OpenArena, perform the following steps:

1. From the command line, enter `startx` to launch the desktop environment.

2. From the desktop, launch the Pi Store application by double-clicking on the Pi Store icon.

3. At the top-right of the application, there will be a **Log In** link. Click on the link and log in with your registered account.

4. Click on **Explore**, then **Games**, and then **Fighting**.

5. Click on the **Open Arena** result.

6. At the application information page, click on the **Download** button on the right-hand side of the screen.

7. OpenArena will automatically download, and a window will appear showing the installation process.

8. Press any button to close the window once it has finished installation.

9. When you click on **Launch** to play the game, your Raspberry Pi will reboot and automatically launch OpenArena on the command line.

For playing a single-player match, perform the following steps:

1. From the **open arena** main menu click on Single Player.
2. Select one of the map icons from the list. The opponents in the arena will be listed at the bottom.
3. Click on **Fight** to load the arena and start the match.

For joining a server, perform the following steps:

1. From the **open arena** main menu, click on **MULTIPLAYER**.
2. Edit your player name and customize your character as needed.
3. Click on **Next**.
4. OpenArena will search for servers on your local network.
5. Click on **Servers** at the top of the screen to change from Local to Internet.
6. Double-click on the server you wish to join.
7. You can also manually select a server by clicking **Specify** and entering in the IP address of the server you wish to join.

For running a server, perform the following steps:

1. From the command line, change into the OpenArena directory by typing `cd /usr/local/bin/indiecity/InstalledApps/openarena/Full/`.
2. Execute the oadedicated script by running `./oadedicated.sh`.
3. After Opening IP Socket appears, press *Enter*.
4. At the `]` prompt, type `map oa_dm3` and press *Enter*.
5. The OpenArena dedicated server will now be running on your local network.

How it works...

OpenArena is a free open source first-person shooter, based off the engine that runs Quake 3 Arena. In 2005, iD Software open sourced iD Tech 3 and freely allowed others to modify, extend, and re-use the code in their own projects. The iD Tech 3 is still considered a very sophisticated game engine, which is why it is a great program to show off the capabilities of the Raspberry Pi. With the settings set to high, you can still expect to get a fast frame rate and smooth gameplay while fighting against 32 other players.

OpenArena was formed to recreate the Quake experience with brand new assets, which would allow anyone to download and play for free.

Other than the new assets and name, the game plays just like the original Quake 3 Arena.

The control scheme is as follows:

▶ WASD keys to move (*W* for up, *S* for down, *A* for strafe left, and *D* for strafe right)
▶ Use your mouse to aim
▶ Left mouse click to fire your weapon
▶ Space bar to jump
▶ Number keys to switch weapons

There's more...

A few useful reference links:

▶ For information on OpenArena go to `http://www.openarena.ws`
▶ For information on iD Software go to `http://www.idsoftware.com`
▶ For information on Quake III Arena Source Code go to `https://github.com/id-Software/Quake-III-Arena`
▶ For Raspberry Pi OpenArena documentation go to `http://store.raspberrypi.com/projects/openarena`

Installing Cave Story (Simple)

This task will describe how to download and install **Cave Story**. It will go on to explain how to run it from the CLI.

Getting ready

You will need:

- A Raspberry Pi
- An SD card with the official Raspberry Pi OS, Raspbian, properly loaded
- A USB keyboard
- A USB mouse
- A 5V 1A power supply with Micro-USB connector
- A network connection
- And a screen hooked up to your Raspberry Pi

How to do it...

1. On the command line, enter `wget https://github.com/vanfanel/cavestory_rpi/archive/master.zip` and press *Enter*.

2. Enter `unzip master.zip`.

3. Change into the unzipped directory by typing `cd cavestory_rpi-master`.

4. Type `./nx` to run Cave Story.

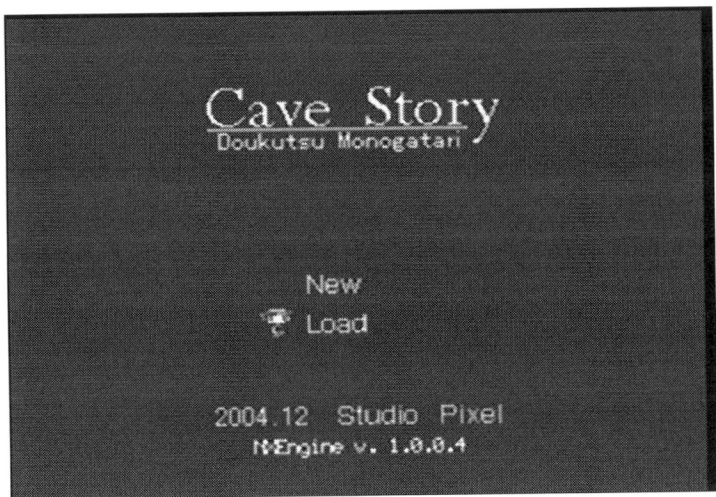

How it works...

Cave Story, also known as **Doukutsu Monogatari**, is a freeware, retro inspired, platforming adventure game. It has been ported to numerous devices, gaming systems, and platforms. NXEngine is an open source clone of the Cave Story engine, and enables you to play Cave Story on Linux and the Raspberry Pi.

The controls are:

- Arrow keys to move
- *Z* to jump
- *X* to fire your weapon
- *A* and S to switch between weapons
- *Q* to show your inventory
- *W* to display your map
- *Esc* to quit

There's more...

A few useful reference links:

- For information on Cave Story go to `http://www.cavestory.org/`
- For information on NX Engine go to `http://nxengine.sourceforge.net/`

Installing Stella (Simple)

This task will describe how to install **Stella**, the Atari 2600 emulator, onto your Raspberry Pi, as well as how to load and play games.

Getting ready

You will need:

- A Raspberry Pi
- An SD card with the official Raspberry Pi OS, Raspbian, properly loaded
- A USB keyboard
- A USB mouse
- A 5V 1A power supply with Micro-USB connector
- A network connection
- And a screen hooked up to your Raspberry Pi

How to do it...

1. On the command line, enter `sudo apt-get install stella` and press *Enter*.

2. Press *y* if asked to continue installing.

3. Type `stella` and press *Enter* to run the emulator.

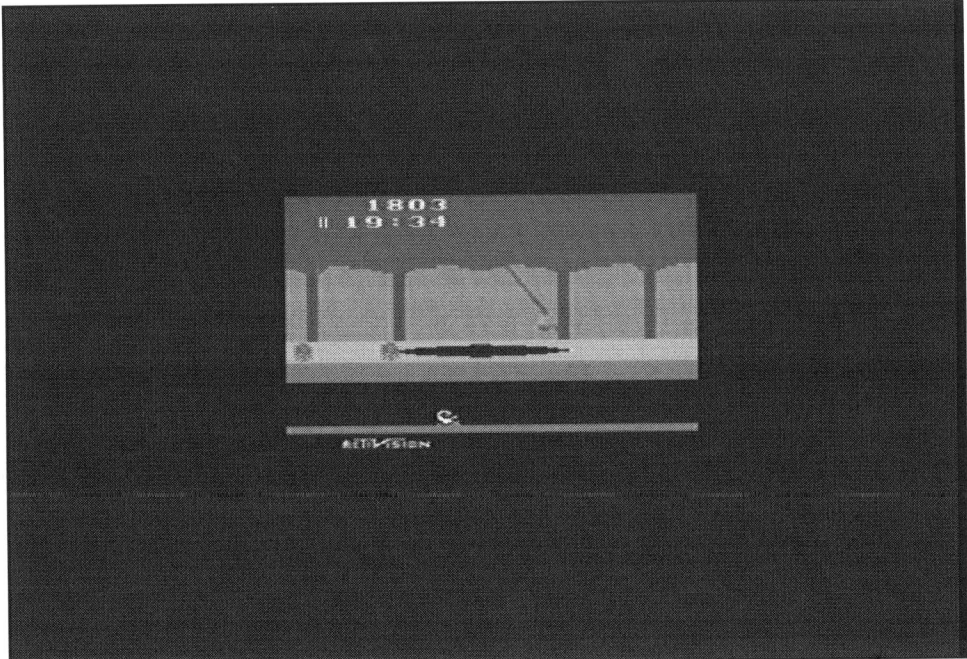

How it works...

The **Atari 2600** is one of the most famous gaming consoles ever made. It started the home console industry and was known for its ports of popular arcade games. It even defined new genres of gaming, such as platforming and action-adventure. Demonstrating its popularity, decades after being manufactured, shows that even now there are developers making games for the system.

Stella is a portable Atari 2600 emulator that has been ported to most architectures and operating systems. It's included in the Raspbian package repository, so all you need to do is install it via `apt-get` for it to be available on your Raspberry Pi.

Stella includes a GUI and allows you to move up and down directories to find your game files.

The controls are:

- Arrow keys to move
- Space bar to fire
- *4* for trigger button
- *5* for booster button
- *F2* to reset the emulated Atari 2600
- *Esc* to return to the menu

There's more...

A few useful reference links:

- For information on Stella go to `http://stella.sourceforge.net/`
- For information on Atari 2600 go to
  `http://en.wikipedia.org/wiki/Atari_2600`
- For information on Atari Age go to `http://atariage.com/`

Using Minecraft Pi Edition (Advanced)

This task will describe how to:

- Download Minecraft Pi Edition
- Install Minecraft
- Create a new Minecraft world
- Use the Minecraft API

Getting ready

You will need:

- A Raspberry Pi
- An SD card with the official Raspberry Pi OS, Raspbian, properly loaded
- A USB keyboard
- A USB mouse
- A 5V 1A power supply with Micro-USB connector
- A network connection
- And a screen hooked up to your Raspberry Pi

How to do it...

For installing and running Minecraft, perform the following steps:

1. Minecraft needs to be run from the GUI environment, so at the command line, type `startx`.

2. From the desktop, double-click on `LXTerminal`.

3. Download Minecraft by typing `wget https://s3.amazonaws.com/assets.minecraft.net/pi/minecraft-pi-0.1.1.tar.gz` into the terminal and pressing *Enter*.

4. Uncompress the file by running `tar zxfv minecraft-pi-0.1.1.tar.gz`.

5. Then change into that directory by typing `cd mcpi`.

6. To run Minecraft type `./minecraft-pi`.

For creating a new Minecraft world, perform the following steps:

1. With Minecraft running, click on **Start Game**.

2. Select **Create New**.

3. After a few moments, you will appear in a brand new Minecraft world environment.

For using the Minecraft Pi Edition Application Programming Interface (API), perform the following steps:

1. In the terminal, you should still be in the `mcpi` folder.
2. Change into the Minecraft Python API folder by typing `cd api/python/mcpi /`.
3. Start the Python interactive shell by running `python` on the terminal.
4. You will see `>>>`, which is where you will enter Python commands.
5. Enter the following commands:

   - `import minecraft`
   - `import block`
   - `mc = minecraft.Minecraft.create()`
   - `mc.postToChat("I am using the API!")`

6. You should now see the `I am using the API` message appear in your Minecraft window.
7. Enter the following commands:

   - `player = mc.player.getPos()`
   - `player`

8. A printout similar to `Vec3(46.0,1.0,-14.0)` should appear.
9. Enter the command `mc.setBlock(player.x +1, player.y, player.z, block.GOLD_BLOCK)`.
10. Directly in front of you a golden block should appear.

How it works...

Minecraft is a sandbox game from **Studio Mojang**. The goal of the game is to create, survive, and have fun. The game is only finished when you say so. The Raspberry Pi version of Minecraft is built on the Pocket Edition engine, which was used to power the Android and iOS version. Because of this, the Raspberry Pi edition can sometimes connect to worlds hosted by cell phones and tablets.

The controls are:

- ▶ Arrows keys to move
- ▶ Mouse movement to look around
- ▶ Left-click to attack or dig
- ▶ Right-click to place a block or eat
- ▶ *E* to open inventory
- ▶ Number keys to select item from main inventory slots
- ▶ Space bar to jump (double jump to fly)

The biggest change that comes with the Raspberry Pi edition is the inclusion of an API. The API allows you to connect to your world with various programming languages, and modify the environment through various commands.

The first step needed to begin using the API is to go into the directory where the Python API files are stored. If you want to make your own programs, you would copy these files to your own project. When you run Python, you are brought into the interactive shell. The `import` command loads the file, otherwise known as a module, into memory and makes its functions available for you to use. Next, load the `minecraft` and `block` modules that will allow you to connect to your running Minecraft game and manipulate the blocks.

Running `mc = minecraft.Minecraft.create()` forms the connection to your Minecraft game and keeps the connection in the variable `mc`. When you want to send a command to your game, you will make use of the `mc` variable, because it's storing all the needed information. The `postToChat()` function sends a line of text to your game's screen. `player.getPos()` gets the current X, Y, and Z coordinates of your character in the game. We then store that into the variable `player`. By typing the variable name into the shell, we can see the current value that it is been stored. In this case, it shows the saved coordinates.

Now that you have the player's coordinates, you can manipulate the world around it. By running `mc.setBlock(1,1,1, block.GOLD_BLOCK)`, a gold block will appear at the coordinates of (1, 1, 1). But let's say you wanted that gold block to appear right in front of your character. You can use the `player` variable, set earlier, to retrieve its coordinates. By entering `mc.setBlock(player.x +1, player.y, player.z, block.GOLD_BLOCK)` in the command line, you are telling the game to place that gold block at the spot in front of the character. If you didn't add `1` to `player.x`, the block would end up in the exact same spot you were in, so move it forward by one to avoid that.

The previous code only scratches the surface of what is available in the API.

There's more...

A few useful reference links:

- For information on Minecraft go to `http://pi.minecraft.net/`
- For information on Minecraft API go to `http://www.raspberrypi.org/archives/3445`
- For information on Python go to `http://www.python.org/`

Staying up-to-date (Intermediate)

This task will describe how to keep the Raspberry Pi operating system up-to-date by using `raspi-config`, `rpi-update`, and `apt-get`.

Getting ready

You will need:

- A Raspberry Pi
- An SD Card with the official Raspberry Pi OS, Raspbian, properly loaded
- A USB keyboard
- A USB mouse
- A 5V 1A power supply with Micro-USB connector
- A network connection
- And a screen hooked up to your Raspberry Pi

How to do it...

1. At the command line, enter `sudo apt-get update`.

2. When that has finished, enter `sudo apt-get upgrade`.

3. Answer yes to any prompts that ask for confirmation.

4. Reboot your Raspberry Pi by entering `sudo reboot`.

5. After logging back in, enter `sudo rpi-update` into the terminal.

6. Select the defaults that are presented.

7. Reboot your Raspberry Pi by entering `sudo reboot`.

8. After logging back in, enter into the terminal `sudo raspi-config`.

9. From the menu, scroll down to the `Update` option, and press *Enter*.

10. When that is complete press the right key to select finish, and press *Enter*.

11. If prompted to reboot, select **Yes**.

12. Your Raspberry Pi operating system, firmware, and configuration panel are now up-to-date.

How it works...

The Advanced Packaging Tool (APT) is a standard package manager for Linux, specifically Debian, which is what Raspbian is built on. A package manager manages all the programs, games, and supporting files (known as dependencies) that are installed into your system. Periodically, the list of new packages is updated, so it is recommended to run apt-get update once a month. We have to use sudo, because apt-get needs to be run as root. An apt-get upgrade checks the list of installed packages against the list of what has been updated, and if it finds anything it will try to upgrade those packages. Running an apt-get upgrade is recommended at least once a month to stay updated against security flaws, exploits, and bug fixes.

Rpi-update is an open source program included in the latest versions of Raspbian that facilitates the easy upgrading of firmware on the Raspberry Pi. The firmware is code that is loaded before the operating system boots, sets all of the hardware up, and activates features on the board. Firmware updates have been released to support newer SD cards, better USB support, more video codecs, faster video performance, as well as other little bug fixes and feature enhancements.

Raspi-config is another open source tool included in all versions of Raspbian. Raspi-config is the first program activated after a successful boot-up on a new installation. The software helps you configure Raspberry Pi to your liking, with options including memory splits, keyboard layout, overclocking, and many other settings. Running the update option will check for and install newer versions of raspi-config, enabling you to access new built-in features of the Raspberry Pi.

There's more...

A few useful reference links:

▸ For information on Advanced Packaging Tool go to `http://wiki.debian.org/Apt`

▸ For information on rpi-update go to `https://github.com/Hexxeh/rpi-update`

▸ For information on raspi-config go to `http://elinux.org/RPi_raspi-config`

Common troubleshooting (Intermediate)

This task will describe various issues that can happen when using the Raspberry Pi including:

▸ Game display issues

▸ Power supply issues

▸ USB issues

How to do it...

The following are a few common issues that you might face and how to resolve them:

▸ EmulationStation returns an error when I try to launch it

Running `sudo apt-get install libsdl1.2-dev libboost-filesystem-dev libfreeimage-dev libfreetype6-dev libsdl-mixer1.2-dev ttf-dejavu` will install the needed dependencies that EmulationStation requires to run.

▸ **Nothing happens when I turn it on**

❑ Make sure the power supply is rated for 5v 1amp

❑ Is the power light illuminated on the Raspberry Pi?

❑ Is the monitor on and the video cable plugged in?

❑ Is the SD card properly formatted?

▸ **Some of the games seem slow**

1. You can overclock your Raspberry Pi to seek out extra performance and speed.

2. Overclocking can corrupt your SD card, requiring you to reload Raspbian on it. If your Raspberry Pi seems to be unresponsive, reboot and hold down the Shift key to temporarily reset the overclock settings.

3. Run raspi-config.

4. Select overclocking.

5. Select the lowest overclock

6. Reboot and check the performance

7. If it is still slow, select the next overclock setting.

8. If the game still runs at an unacceptable performance, the best bet is to post to the Raspberry Pi forums. As the Raspberry Pi platform matures, new enhancements and performance tweaks will be available.

▸ Connecting via HDMI doesn't work

1. Edit the `config.txt` file and set `hdmi_safe=1`.

2. Turn the TV on before turning on the Raspberry Pi.

How it works...

EmulationStation, as well as other games, might require dependencies that have not been loaded during installation. `libsdl1.2-dev`, `libboost-filesystem-dev`, `libfreeimage-dev`, `libfreetype6-dev`, `libsdl-mixer1.2-dev`, and `ttf-dejavu` are common libraries that are used in a number of games that might not have been installed, or need to be updated.

Most of the reasons a Raspberry Pi will fail to boot or experience problems during use are because of an inadequate power supply. Many Micro-USB chargers are manufactured with minimal quality assurance, so if you do experience issues, the first thing to do would be to try a different brand of charger. Most branded cell phone chargers will properly power a Raspberry Pi.

If that doesn't fix the issue, the next step is to test out the SD card. A properly formatted SD card will have a small *boot* drive that is readable by Windows and Mac OS X operating systems. If you cannot see the boot drive or any files inside it, most likely your SD card hasn't been properly imaged.

The boot drive contains a text file named `config.txt`. This file stores all the configuration parameters and is read each time your Raspberry Pi powers on. Editing this file allows you to fine-tune your Raspberry Pi and can also help in resolving various issues that can crop up during use.

The Raspberry Pi, by default, runs at 700 MHz, but has the capability to be overclocked to a higher speed. Most Raspberry Pis have been noted as to be working fine at 900 MHz and some even higher than 1 GHz. Overclocking the CPU with raspi-config automatically throttles the speed as needed, so when not in use, it reduces power down to 700 MHz. Even with the throttle, overclocking can make your system unstable and can corrupt the SD card. If your system fails to boot after overclocking, holding down *Shift* will try to turn off the overclocking in software. If that does not work, you can edit the `config.txt` file and set `arm_freq=700` to disable overclocking. If all else fails, you can re-image your SD card. All overclocking information is stored in `config.txt`, and re-imaging your card will reset it.

If you have trouble getting an image to appear on your TV through HDMI, the most common fix is to edit `config.txt` and set `hdmi_safe=1`. This changes and boosts the HDMI signal, so that it is more likely to sync with your TV. Another simple change is to make sure that the TV is on and connected before you power on the Raspberry Pi.

There's more...

A few useful reference links:

- For information on Element 14 / Newark Raspberry Pi accessories go to `http://www.newark.com/raspberrypi`

- For information on the Pi-Hut Preloaded SD cards go to `http://thepihut.com/`

- For information on E-Linux RPi troubleshooting guide go to `http://elinux.org/R-Pi_Troubleshooting`

- For information on E-Linux RPi Config guide go to `http://elinux.org/RPi_config.txt`

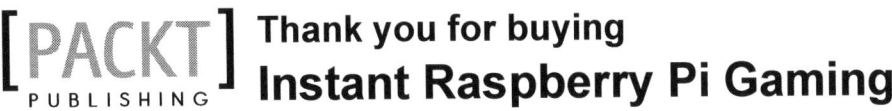

About Packt Publishing

Packt, pronounced 'packed', published its first book "*Mastering phpMyAdmin for Effective MySQL Management*" in April 2004 and subsequently continued to specialize in publishing highly focused books on specific technologies and solutions.

Our books and publications share the experiences of your fellow IT professionals in adapting and customizing today's systems, applications, and frameworks. Our solution based books give you the knowledge and power to customize the software and technologies you're using to get the job done. Packt books are more specific and less general than the IT books you have seen in the past. Our unique business model allows us to bring you more focused information, giving you more of what you need to know, and less of what you don't.

Packt is a modern, yet unique publishing company, which focuses on producing quality, cutting-edge books for communities of developers, administrators, and newbies alike. For more information, please visit our website: www.packtpub.com.

Writing for Packt

We welcome all inquiries from people who are interested in authoring. Book proposals should be sent to author@packtpub.com. If your book idea is still at an early stage and you would like to discuss it first before writing a formal book proposal, contact us; one of our commissioning editors will get in touch with you.

We're not just looking for published authors; if you have strong technical skills but no writing experience, our experienced editors can help you develop a writing career, or simply get some additional reward for your expertise.

Instant Minecraft: Pi Edition Coding How-to

ISBN: 978-1-783280-63-6   Paperback: 50 pages

Expand your Minecraft world by learning to code with Minecraft: Pi Edition

1. Learn something new in an Instant! A short, fast, focused guide delivering immediate results

2. Enhance your Minecraft building techniques using computer code

3. Get started with the Linux operating system on the Raspberry Pi

4. Make the Minecraft world interact with the real world

Raspberry Pi Networking Cookbook

ISBN: 978-1-849694-60-5   Paperback: 204 pages

An epic collection of practical and engaging recipes for the Raspberry Pi!

1. Learn how to install, administer, and maintain your Raspberry Pi

2. Create a network fileserver for sharing documents, music, and videos

3. Host a web portal, collaboration wiki, or even your own wireless access point

4. Connect to your desktop remotely, with minimum hassle

Please check **www.PacktPub.com** for information on our titles

Raspberry Pi Media Center

ISBN: 978-1-782163-02-2   Paperback: 108 pages

Transform your Raspberry Pi into a full-blown media center within 24 hours

1. Discover how you can stream video, music, and photos straight to your TV

2. Play existing content from your computer or USB drive

3. Watch and record TV via satellite, cable, or terrestrial

4. Build your very own library that automatically includes detailed information and cover material

Raspberry Pi for Secret Agents

ISBN: 978-1-849695-78-7   Paperback: 152 pages

Turn your Raspberry Pi into your very own secret agent toolbox with this set of exciting projects!

1. Detect an intruder on camera and set off an alarm

2. Listen in or record conversations from a distance

3. Find out what the other computers on your network are up to

4. Unleash your Raspberry Pi on the world

Please check **www.PacktPub.com** for information on our titles

Made in the USA
Lexington, KY
16 December 2013